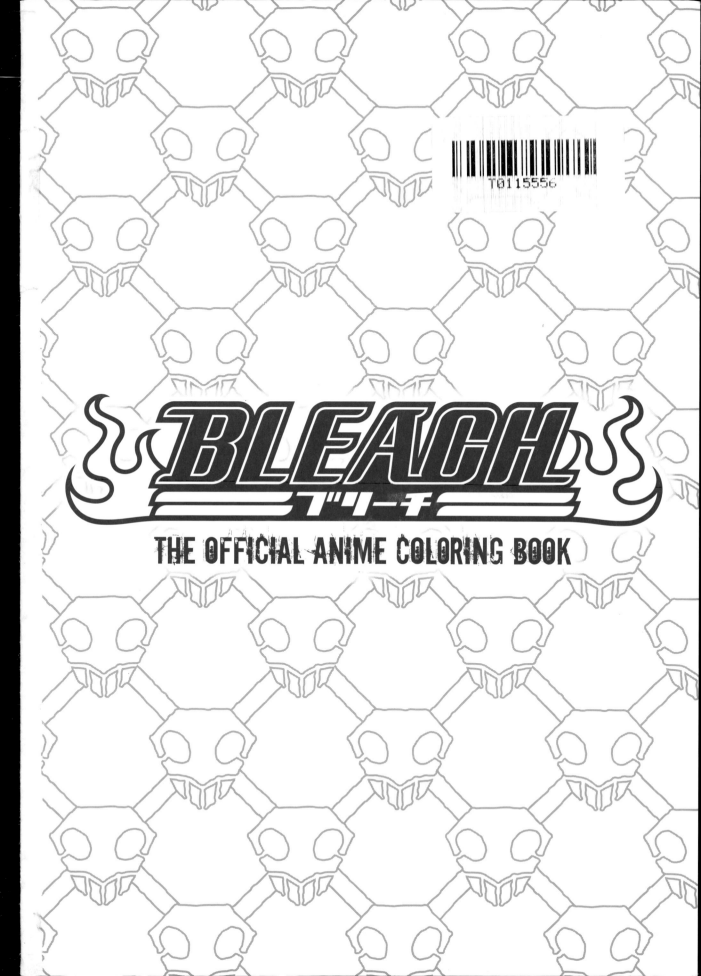

BLEACH
ブリーチ

THE OFFICIAL ANIME COLORING BOOK

T0115556

**BLEACH: THE OFFICIAL
ANIME COLORING BOOK**

© Tite Kubo/Shueisha, TV TOKYO, dentsu, Pierrot

DESIGN **IAN MILLER**   EDITOR **AMANDA NG**

The stories, characters, and incidents mentioned
in this publication are entirely fictional.

No portion of this book may be reproduced or transmitted in
any form or by any means without written permission from
the copyright holders.

Printed in the U.S.A.

ISBN: 978-1-9747-4091-8

Published by VIZ Media, LLC
P.O. Box 77010
San Francisco, CA 94107

10 9 8 7 6 5 4 3 2 1
First printing, September 2023

viz.com

© Tite Kubo/Shueisha, TV TOKYO, dentsu, Pierrot

© Tite Kubo/Shueisha, TV TOKYO, dentsu, Pierrot

© Tite Kubo/Shueisha, TV TOKYO, dentsu, Pierrot

© Tite Kubo/Shueisha, TV TOKYO, dentsu, Pierrot

© Tite Kubo/Shueisha, TV TOKYO, dentsu, Pierrot

© Tite Kubo/Shueisha, TV TOKYO, dentsu, Pierrot

© Tite Kubo/Shueisha, TV TOKYO, dentsu, Pierrot

© Tite Kubo/Shueisha, TV TOKYO, dentsu, Pierrot

© Tite Kubo/Shueisha, TV TOKYO, dentsu, Pierrot

© Tite Kubo/Shueisha, TV TOKYO, dentsu, Pierrot

© Tite Kubo/Shueisha, TV TOKYO, dentsu, Pierrot

© Tite Kubo/Shueisha, TV TOKYO, dentsu, Pierrot

© Tite Kubo/Shueisha, TV TOKYO, dentsu, Pierrot

© Tite Kubo/Shueisha, TV TOKYO, dentsu, Pierrot

© Tite Kubo/Shueisha, TV TOKYO, dentsu, Pierrot

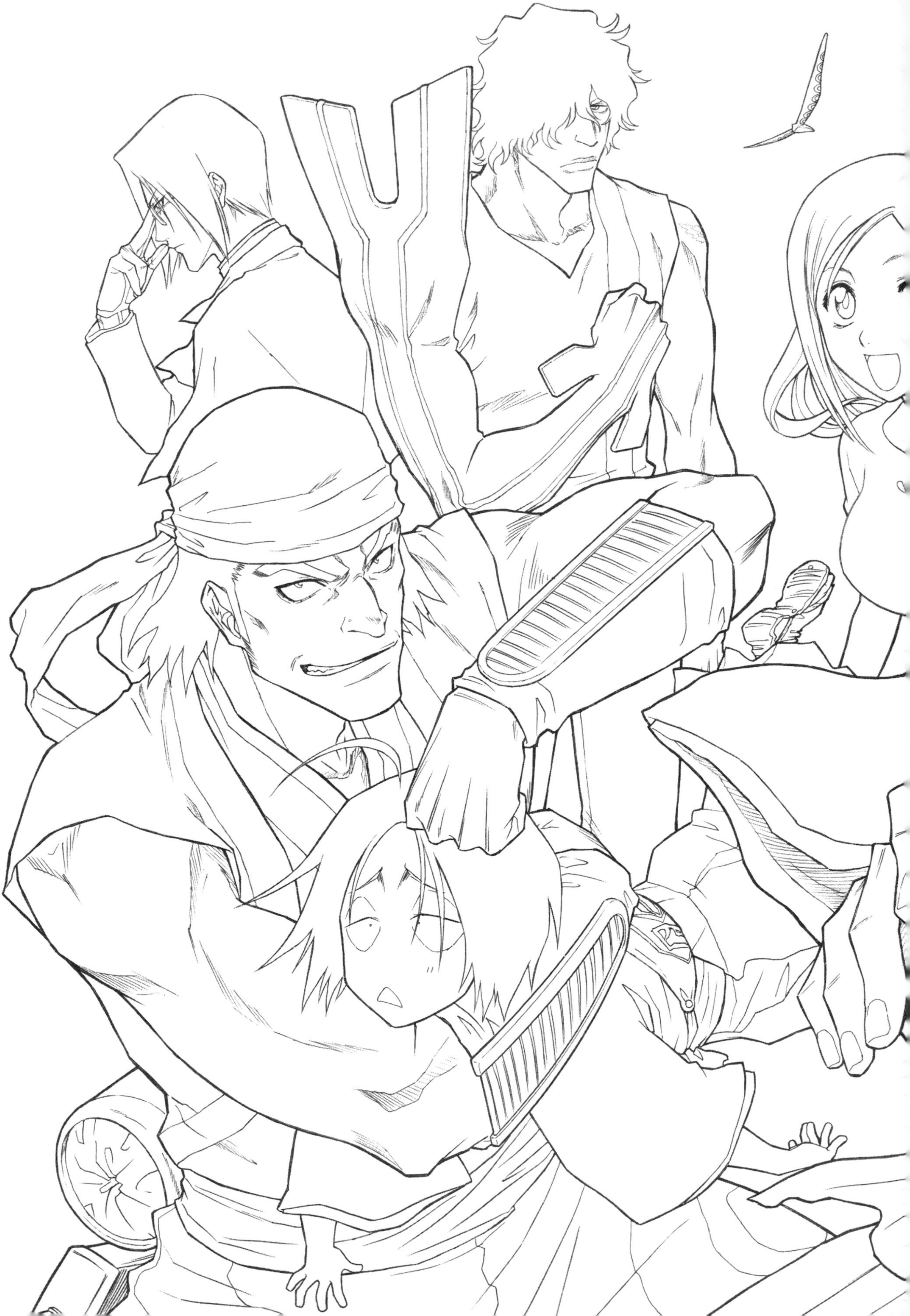

© Tite Kubo/Shueisha, TV TOKYO, dentsu, Pierrot

© Tite Kubo/Shueisha, TV TOKYO, dentsu, Pierrot

© Tite Kubo/Shueisha, TV TOKYO, dentsu, Pierrot

© Tite Kubo/Shueisha, TV TOKYO, dentsu, Pierrot

© Tite Kubo/Shueisha, TV TOKYO, dentsu, Pierrot

© Tite Kubo/Shueisha, TV TOKYO, dentsu, Pierrot

© Tite Kubo/Shueisha, TV TOKYO, dentsu, Pierrot

© Tite Kubo/Shueisha, TV TOKYO, dentsu, Pierrot

© Tite Kubo/Shueisha, TV TOKYO, dentsu, Pierrot

© Tite Kubo/Shueisha, TV TOKYO, dentsu, Pierrot

© Tite Kubo/Shueisha, TV TOKYO, dentsu, Pierrot

© Tite Kubo/Shueisha, TV TOKYO, dentsu, Pierrot

© Tite Kubo/Shueisha, TV TOKYO, dentsu, Pierrot

© Tite Kubo/Shueisha, TV TOKYO, dentsu, Pierrot

© Tite Kubo/Shueisha, TV TOKYO, dentsu, Pierrot

© Tite Kubo/Shueisha, TV TOKYO, dentsu, Pierrot

© Tite Kubo/Shueisha, TV TOKYO, dentsu, Pierrot

© Tite Kubo/Shueisha, TV TOKYO, dentsu, Pierrot

© Tite Kubo/Shueisha, TV TOKYO, dentsu, Pierrot

© Tite Kubo/Shueisha, TV TOKYO, dentsu, Pierrot

© Tite Kubo/Shueisha, TV TOKYO, dentsu, Pierrot

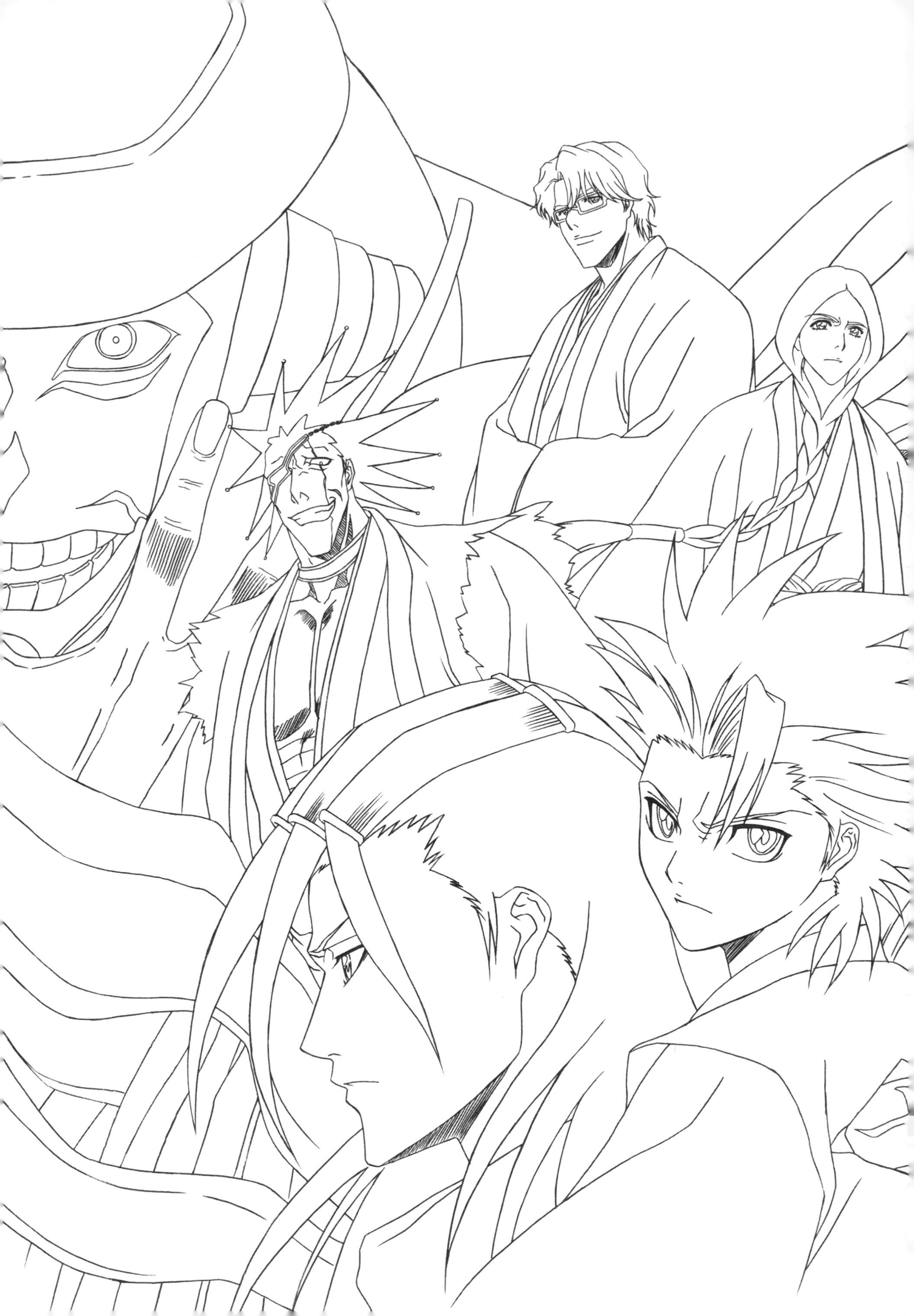

© Tite Kubo/Shueisha, TV TOKYO,.dentsu, Pierrot

© Tite Kubo/Shueisha, TV TOKYO, dentsu, Pierrot

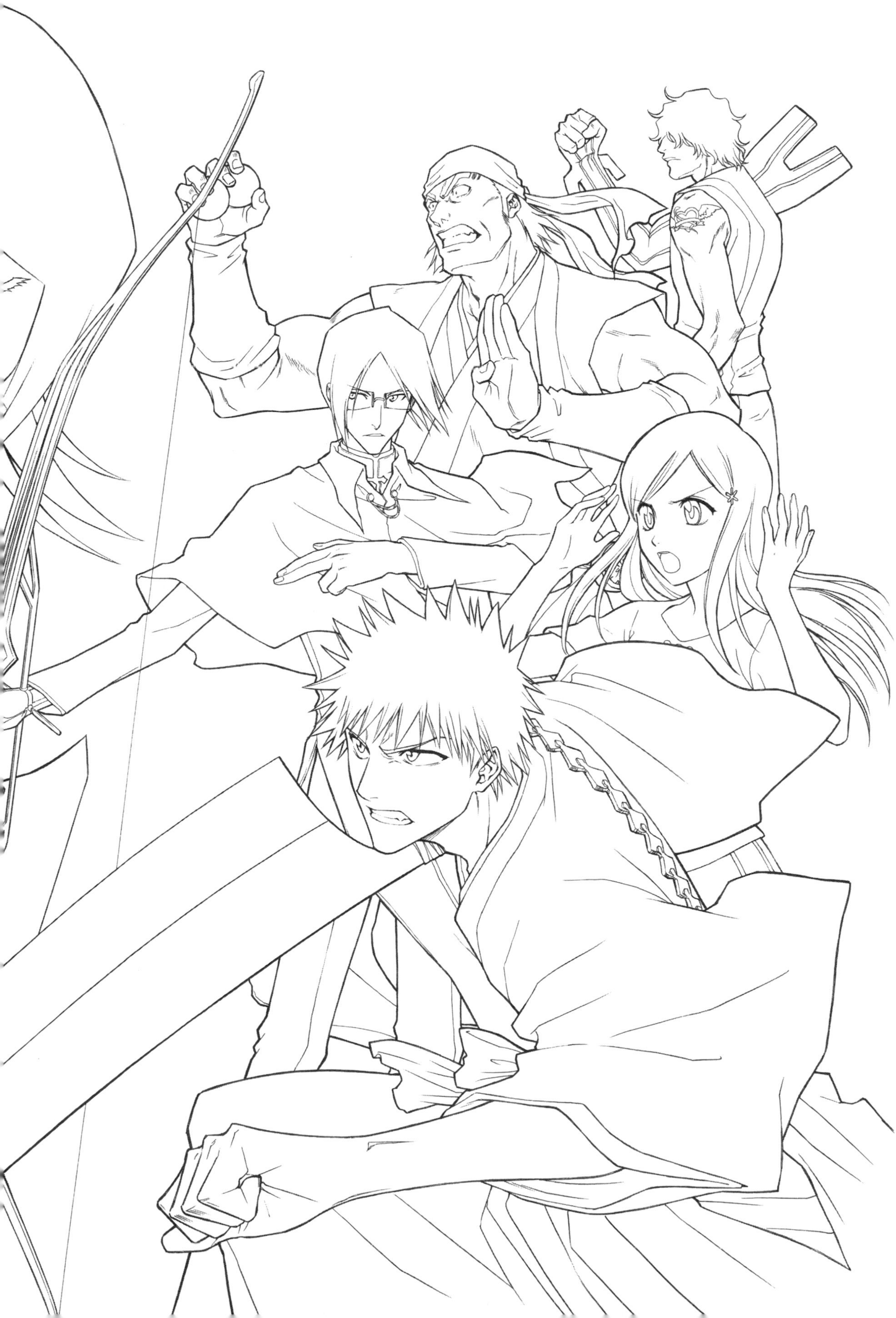

© Tite Kubo/Shueisha, TV TOKYO, dentsu, Pierrot

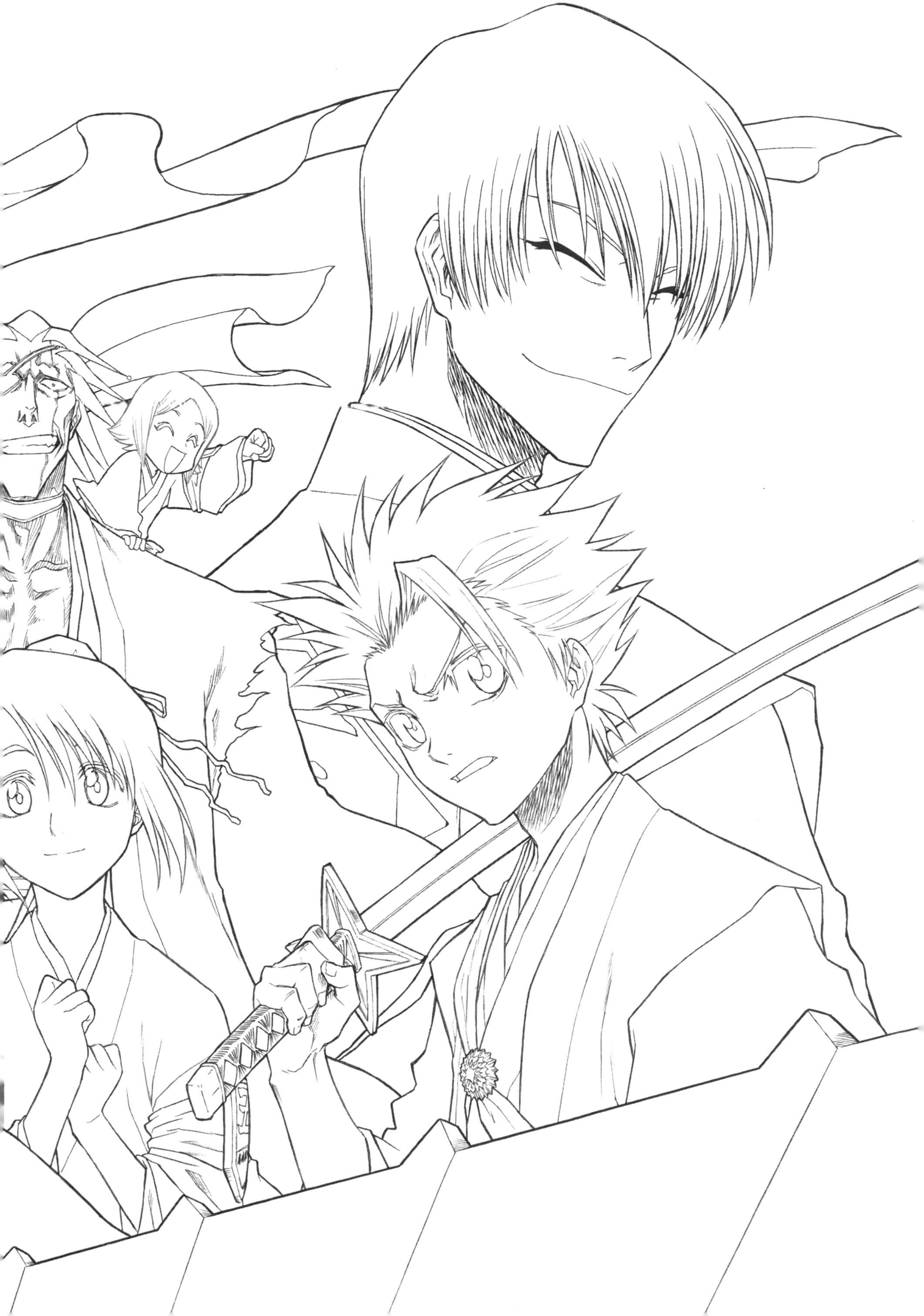

© Tite Kubo/Shueisha, TV TOKYO, dentsu, Pierrot

© Tite Kubo/Shueisha, TV TOKYO, dentsu, Pierrot

© Tite Kubo/Shueisha, ,TV TOKYO, dentsu, Pierrot

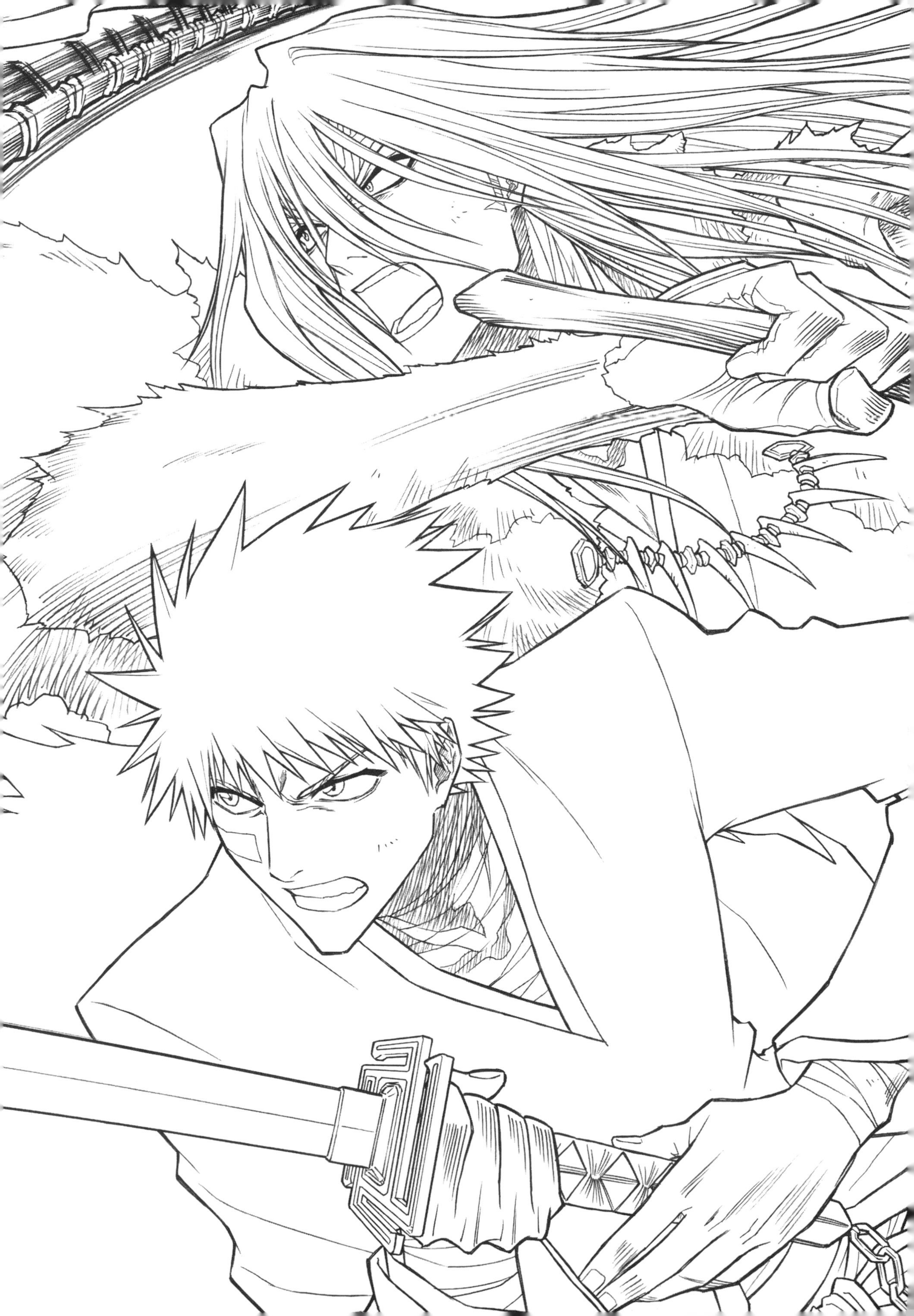

© Tite Kubo/Shueisha, TV TOKYO, dentsu, Pierrot

© Tite Kubo/Shueisha, TV TOKYO, dentsu, Pierrot

© Tite Kubo/Shueisha, TV TOKYO, dentsu, Pierrot

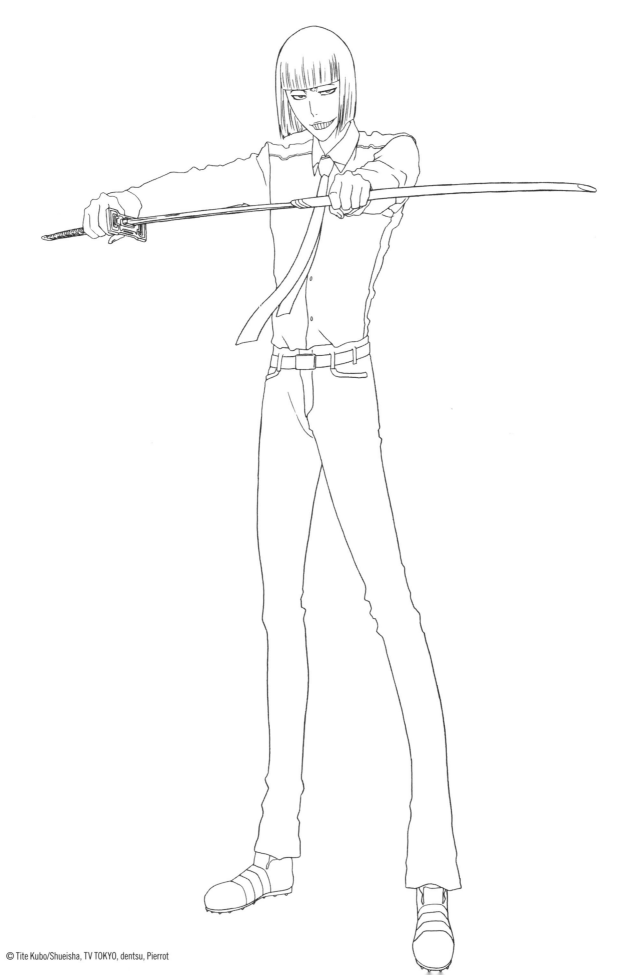

© Tite Kubo/Shueisha, TV TOKYO, dentsu, Pierrot

© Tite Kubo/Shueisha, TV TOKYO, dentsu, Pierrot

© Tite Kubo/Shueisha, TV TOKYO, dentsu, Pierrot

© Tite Kubo/Shueisha, TV TOKYO, dentsu, Pierrot

© Tite Kubo/Shueisha, TV TOKYO, dentsu, Pierrot

© Tite Kubo/Shueisha, TV TOKYO, dentsu, Pierrot

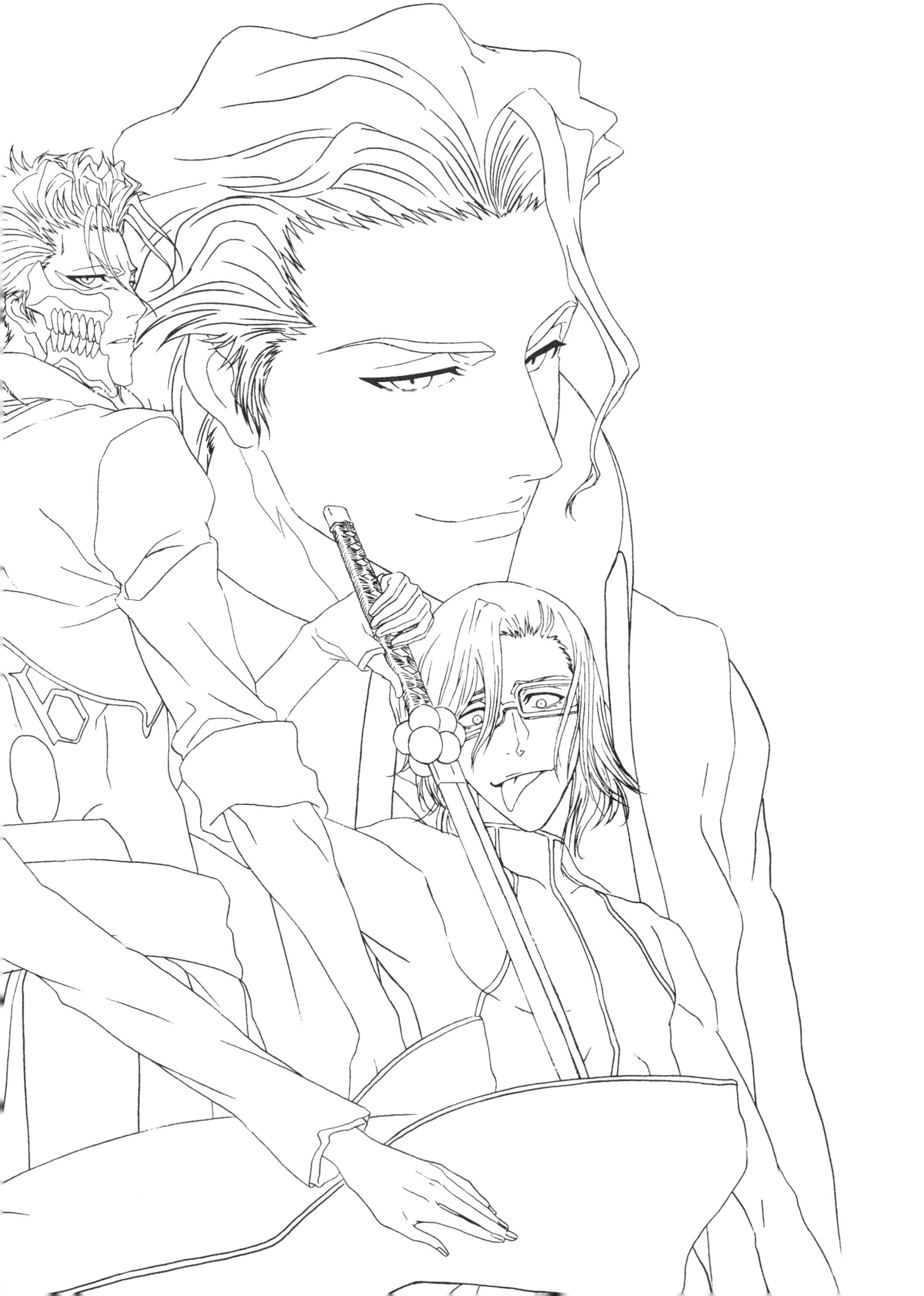

© Tite Kubo/Shueisha, TV TOKYO, dentsu, Pierrot

© Tite Kubo/Shueisha, TV TOKYO, dentsu, Pierrot

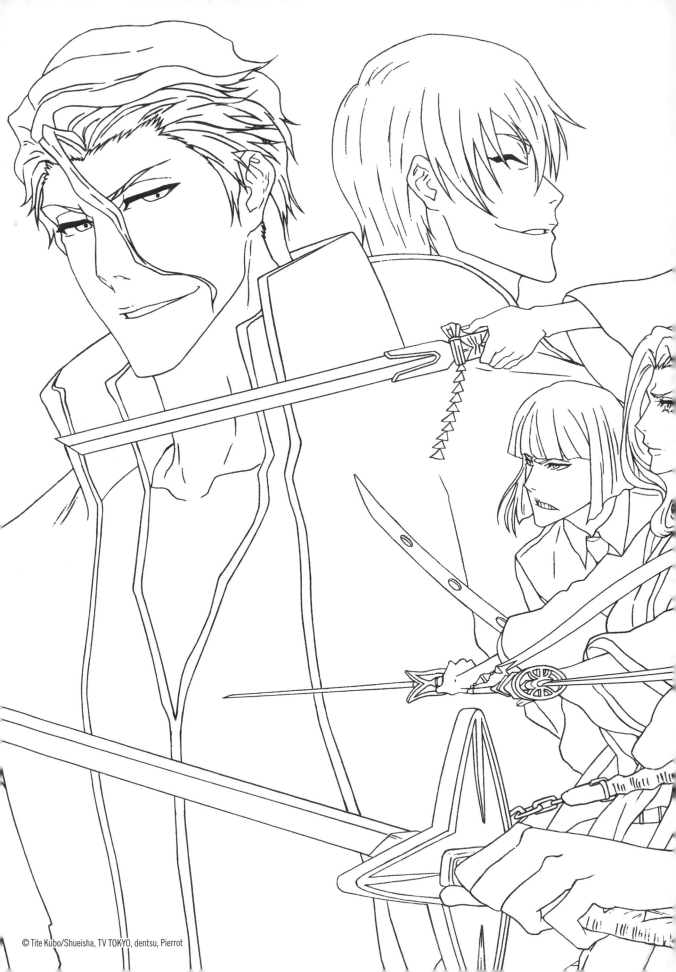

© Tite Kubo/Shueisha, TV TOKYO, dentsu, Pierrot

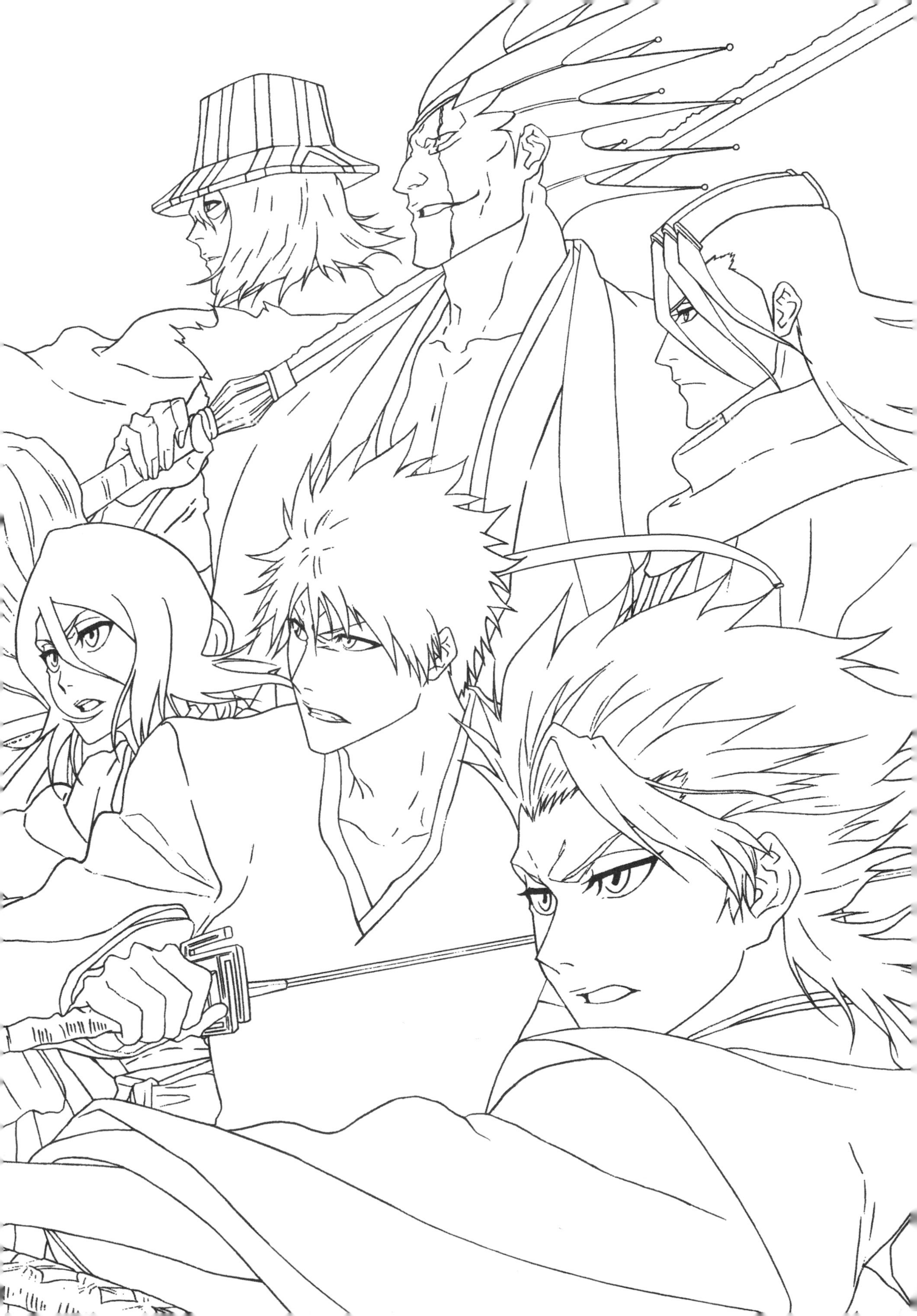

© Tite Kubo/Shueisha, TV TOKYO, dentsu, Pierrot

© Tite Kubo/Shueisha, TV TOKYO, dentsu, Pierrot

© Tite Kubo/Shueisha, TV TOKYO, dentsu, Pierrot

© Tite Kubo/Shueisha, TV TOKYO, dentsu, Pierrot

© Tite Kubo/Shueisha, TV TOKYO, dentsu, Pierrot

© Tite Kubo/Shueisha, TV TOKYO, dentsu, Pierrot

© Tite Kubo/Shueisha, TV TOKYO, dentsu, Pierrot

© Tite Kubo/Shueisha, TV TOKYO, dentsu, Pierrot

© Tite Kubo/Shueisha, TV TOKYO, dentsu, Pierrot

© Tite Kubo/Shueisha, TV TOKYO, dentsu, Pierrot

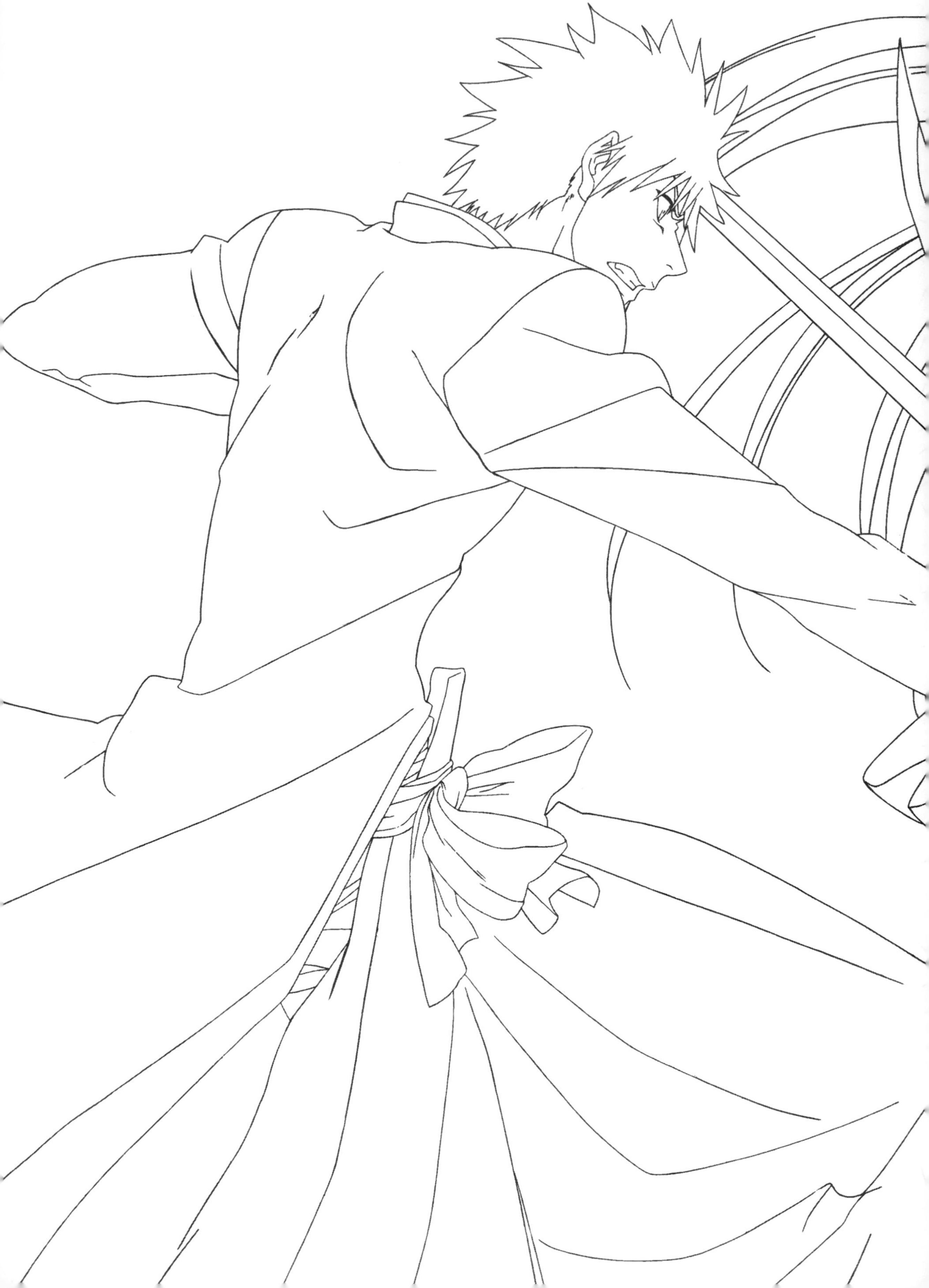

© Tite Kubo/Shueisha, TV TOKYO, dentsu, Pierrot

© Tite Kubo/Shueisha, TV TOKYO, dentsu, Pierrot

© Tite Kubo/Shueisha, TV TOKYO, dentsu, Pierrot

© Tite Kubo/Shueisha, TV TOKYO, dentsu, Pierrot

© Tite Kubo/Shueisha, TV TOKYO, dentsu, Pierrot

© Tite Kubo/Shueisha, TV TOKYO, dentsu, Pierrot